SURVIVAL GUIDE FOR
COLLEGE STUDENTS
WITH
ADHD or LD

SECOND EDITION

Published by
MAGINATION PRESS
An Educational Publishing Foundation Book
American Psychological Association
750 First Street, NE
Washington, DC 20002

For more information about our books, including a complete catalog, please write to us,
call 1-800-374-2721, or visit our website at www.maginationpress.com.

Editor: Kristine Enderle
Art Director: Susan K. White

Library of Congress Cataloging-in-Publication Data

Nadeau, Kathleen G.
Survival guide for college students with ADHD or LD / Kathleen G. Nadeau.– 2nd ed.
p. cm.
Title of 1st ed.: Survival guide for college students with ADD or LD.
"An Educational Publishing Foundation book."
ISBN 1-59147-388-8 (hardcover : alk. paper) – ISBN 1-59147-389-6 (pbk. : alk. paper)
1. Learning disabled–Education (Higher)–United States.
2. Attention-deficit-disordered youth–Education (Higher)–United States.
3. College student orientation–United States. 4. College choice–United States.
I. Nadeau, Kathleen G. Survival guide for college students with ADD or LD. II. Title.

LC4818.5.N33 2006
371.9'0474–dc22

2005027891

10 9 8 7 6 5 4 3 2 1

SURVIVAL GUIDE FOR

COLLEGE STUDENTS

WITH

ADHD OR LD

SECOND EDITION

by Kathleen G. Nadeau, Ph.D.

MAGINATION PRESS • WASHINGTON, D.C.

CONTENTS

CHAPTER 3
HELP IN THE COMMUNITY

If you are a high school student with ADHD/LD and you are getting ready to apply to college, or if you are a college student with ADHD/LD, this guide can help you survive and succeed in school. Although a number of books address college students with ADHD/LD, this slim volume is the book of choice for many because it is "ADHD/LD-friendly," meaning that it is brief, readable, and chock-full of practical advice to help you deal with the challenges of ADHD or LD.

The *Survival Guide for College Students with ADHD or LD* also looks at the positive aspects of ADHD. It helps you recognize your strengths, many of which are directly related to ADHD: curiosity, energy, enthusiasm, and a drive that can lead to great success when focused in a positive direction.

Success in college for students with learning or attention problems requires a working partnership between you and your college. You will need to be informed about your learning style and about specific problem areas that require accommodations. This book is designed to help you gain that information, to find the support you need, and to become an effective self-advocate.

NOTE: This book was written for students with Attention Deficit Hyperactivity Disorder (ADHD) and /or learning disabilities (LD) who are applying to college, or who may already be enrolled in college. In general, the term "ADHD/LD" is used throughout the book. The terms "ADHD" and "LD" are used separately only when the topic clearly applies to just one or the other.

There has never been a better time for students with ADHD/LD to attend college. Awareness of ADHD has grown tremendously in recent years. As a result, knowledge of how to help students with ADHD/LD is much greater. In the early 1990s, many colleges and universities were only beginning to develop ADHD/LD support services as required by law for all schools receiving federal funding. Now, many campuses have well-developed support programs and are proficient at helping students with ADHD/LD succeed. The result? Increasing numbers of college students with ADHD/LD are graduating from college and going on to graduate school or to successful careers.

Still, some colleges are better equipped to serve you than others. This book explains how to evaluate colleges (or the school you currently attend) to determine which ones can provide the services and support you'll need.

Tips and advice gathered from college students like yourself, as well as from ADHD/LD specialists, will show you how to succeed in college. So grab this survival guide and keep it handy for ready reference. The keys to your success are waiting inside!

CHAPTER 1

CHOOSING A COLLEGE THAT'S RIGHT FOR YOU

The first key to college success is to make a good college choice. This chapter gives you guidelines for choosing a college that's a good match for you. It also talks about how to assess ADHD/LD support services and to find an ADHD/LD-friendly college. In the resources section at the back of this book, a number of college guides are listed that may be helpful to you as you gather information about schools.

GETTING STARTED

With more than 3,000 colleges and universities in the United States, many students and parents feel overwhelmed as they begin to think about college. Sometimes when an individual feels overwhelmed by too many choices, the reaction is to make a choice too quickly, with too little information, or to fall back on easy choices.

This chapter will guide you (and your parents) step-by-step through the process of narrowing your choices systematically. You'll be able to move from a path of "too many choices" to one of a few good choices, building a list of colleges along the way that will be a good match for your needs and preferences.

To reach your short list of good choices, keep the following guidelines in mind.

GUIDELINE 1
Seek guidance and support

Don't try to do it all alone. Ultimately it is your decision where to go to college, but you will benefit from asking for assistance and advice. Don't be shy or embarrassed about asking!

You can start by bouncing ideas off your parents and friends. Teachers are good sources of information too. School counselors, specialized college counselors, and college guidebooks can also help you make good choices.

If you have specific needs or concerns, you might consider using a specialized college counselor. In response to the growing number of college applicants with ADHD or LD, many private college counselors have developed specialties in advising these students. Although such services come at a price, the expense may be an excellent investment when you consider the high cost of college—and choosing the wrong one for you.

GUIDELINE 2
Get an early start

Start the college selection process early during your junior year (if not sooner). A good place to begin is by talking to the college guidance counselor at your school. These services are free, and can help you start building a list of colleges to consider.

Many colleges and universities send recruiters to high schools early in the school year too. By making preliminary choices, you can attend the recruiting sessions for the schools you are interested in.

With at least a year to gather information, you will be able to thoroughly research schools, services, and programs, and make an informed decision. Additionally, you will have plenty of time to complete applications and decide which college to attend.

GUIDELINE 3
Determine your needs

Assess the level of support you will need in college, with guidance from your school counselor or an educational professional. There are several levels of support available in college:

- Specialized schools that specifically serve students with ADHD or LD.

- Schools with separate intensive support programs for which you pay a fee in addition to your regular tuition.

- Schools that offer special supports for entering freshmen, such as a summer orientation program before classes begin in the fall.

- Schools with a formal ADHD or LD support office that provide counselors or coaches with specialized training.

- Schools whose support for students with ADHD or LD is basic or meets the minimum requirements, with few or no counselors trained to work with students with ADHD or LD.

Different students need different levels of support. If you have significant difficulties with reading, writing, or math, you may do better in a school with an intensive support program. If you do not have learning disabilities, or if you have been able to succeed fairly well in high school, you may need only the types of supports and accommodations that are standard on most college campuses.

With the help of these guidelines, your goal will be to develop a list of colleges to investigate more closely.

ASSESSING ADHD OR LD SUPPORT SERVICES

Every college is required by law to provide accommodations to students with ADHD or LD. An "accommodation" is an alteration in procedure made to accommodate your specific learning needs. All campuses provide basic accommodations, but some schools go far beyond what is required by law, and will have tremendous resources available for you. Some campuses provide a learning support center that is staffed by several counselors who have specialized training in working with college students with learning or attention problems. Other schools may have only a single person or only a part-time person responsible for all student disability support services.

How can you find out whether a school provides good support services? Ask questions! Here are some questions you can ask, either by phone or by e-mail. By using this list, you and your parents can identify colleges that will match the level of support you need, and help you select colleges to which you may want to apply. As you narrow your choices, you will visit the student support services office of each campus you are considering; there you can ask questions in person and learn much more.

Be careful when consulting specialized college guides (such as those listed in the resource section in the back of this book). Many schools with excellent support services are not included in these specialized guides. Additionally the quality of support services changes from year to year as funding increases or decreases and as support center staff members change. Your best bet is to investigate these services yourself, using the following questions as a guide.

QUESTIONS TO ASK AT THE ACADEMIC COUNSELING
OR STUDENT SUPPORT SERVICES OFFICE

QUALITY

Q *Is there a distinct student support services office staffed by a director and other counselors?*

Some campuses provide an entire learning support center dedicated to assisting students with learning or attention problems. This center acts as an academic counseling office, tutoring center, social support network, and repository for information on classes, professors, programs, and community services. This type of support center is the best bet.

At the other end of the spectrum, some schools provide a single individual or the part-time services of an individual working out of the dean's office or counseling center. Still, this individual may have experience with ADHD or LD students and be supportive of your needs.

Q *Does the director of student support services have specialized training in ADHD and LD?*

Ideally you'd like the director of student support services to have specialized training in ADHD or LD. However, on some campuses the director of disability support services is a specialist with expertise in working with a variety of disabled students, including those who are hearing impaired, blind, or physically disabled. Although a director who has little or no training in ADHD or LD can be sympathetic to your needs, it is to your advantage to receive support services from a program directed by a specialist in ADHD and LD issues.

Q How many students with ADHD or LD are registered with the support services office?

Strong programs will typically have a large number of students registered for their services. The number of students is an excellent indicator of the level of support a school provides. It also indicates that an ADHD student is more likely to be at that school.

Q How long has the support program for students with ADHD/LD existed?

Often the best programs are those of long standing. Although it's possible to develop a good program in a short period of time, it's more likely that well-established programs will offer the highest quality of support.

Q Are there services developed specifically for ADHD students?

Some programs group all students with ADHD and LD together. Although the overlap may be beneficial to all, college students with ADHD have needs specific to ADHD. For example, ADHD coaching assists students with organization and time management. ADHD education programs instruct faculty members to be more aware of the difficulties many students with ADHD have in completing projects and meeting deadlines.

Q Is ADHD coaching available?

A handful of campuses provide ADHD coaching as a support for students, whether free or for a fee. If there are no coaches available on campus, ask if the student support services office maintains a list of private recommended ADHD coaches. A coach can be a great help and worth the investment.

Q Is it possible to interview students on campus with ADHD/LD?

A good way to assess support services quickly is to speak with several students on campus with ADHD/LD. Such meetings may take place informally, by visiting the support services office and speaking to students who are in the office at the time of your visit. Otherwise, ask the director if you could talk to (or e-mail) a current student.

LEVEL OF CAMPUS SUPPORT

Q Are there ADHD or LD student support groups on campus?

A support group can be a valuable resource for students with ADHD/LD because it provides an opportunity to meet other students with similar needs and challenges. Students can provide one another with camaraderie and emotional support as well as study strategies and recommendations about classes and professors.

Are there seminars or classes devoted to teaching study skills to students with ADHD or LD?

Often, students with ADHD or LD need assistance in "learning how to learn." Many students with ADHD/LD have relied on their intelligence and last-minute efforts to make it through high school. Typically, these approaches no longer work in college, where demands for reading and writing increase. A specialized study-skills class can help students learn how to study efficiently, how to combat distractions, and how to acquire test-taking skills.

Do support services staff provide ongoing ADHD or LD guidance or career counseling, and support for those who request it?

Many support services offices are staffed with several counselors or advisors who can meet regularly with students to provide advice, support, and guidance. Ask how frequently meetings can be made or if students can drop in for quick counseling as needed. This will allow you to quickly assess the amount of support available and how easily you can arrange it.

Are academic advisors with a specialized background in ADHD or LD provided for students who qualify for support services?

It is ideal to have an academic advisor who is also an ADHD/LD specialist. Such an advisor may be better able to advise you, help you determine how many courses to take, and which courses to take each term in order not to overload your schedule.

INTENSIVE SUPPORT PROGRAMS

Q *Is there a separate LD support program for students on campus? Must a student apply separately to this program? How is this program designed or structured? Are there extra charges for the program?*

If you and your parents feel that you will be more successful with the extra assistance of a separate intensive support program, these are the questions to ask. It's possible that you may need such programs only during your freshman and sophomore years. Later, if you feel you no longer need this higher level of support, you can move to the support offered through the general academic counseling office.

CLASSROOM ACCOMMODATIONS

Q *Is extended time on exams available to students with ADHD/LD?*

This support is standard on almost all college campuses; however, you will need test documentation stating that you require extended time. Some colleges make distinctions, allowing a student 1.5 times the standard time, 2.0 times the standard time, or unlimited time depending upon test documentation and upon the policies of the individual college.

Q *Are students allowed to take exams in a quiet, nondistracting environment outside the classroom setting?*

Most colleges offer this accommodation. In some instances, the procedure is quite formal and a student must arrange for this accommodation before each exam. Some colleges and professors will allow a more informal arrangement, allowing a student to take the exam in an empty classroom across the hall or in the professor's office.

Q *Is it possible to take all exams on computers?*

This is an important accommodation for students with ADHD/LD whose handwriting is poor and barely legible, or whose spelling ability is limited. Neat, legible exam responses that have been spell-checked on the computer will make a far better impression on a professor or teaching assistant who is grading your exam.

Q *May students ask to be tested in an alternative mode such as a verbal exam, an essay exam, or a take-home exam?*

This accommodation is much less universal, but it is still well worth requesting. Often such an accommodation is up to the discretion of individual professors.

Q *What is the procedure for arranging alternative testing accommodations? Can a student make a single request that applies to all exams during the term?*

Although test accommodations are available on nearly all campuses, the procedure for obtaining these accommodations can be difficult and cumbersome. Find out what procedure you'll need to follow and determine if this will work for you.

Q *Do students with ADHD or LD have early registration privileges?*

Early registration is a valuable accommodation that allows a student to choose the classes or professors most suitable in regard to scheduling, ADHD/LD-friendly courses, and workload or assignments. This greatly enhances classroom success.

Q *Are note-takers available in every class for students who need them?*

A note-taking service is a big plus for ADHD or LD students. It is best if these note-takers are provided in a private, discreet fashion that will not embarrass or draw attention to the student receiving the accommodation. Alternatively, many classes offer course packets with outlines, notes, and study guides. Arrangements sometimes may be made to receive lecture notes from the professor.

Q *Is it possible to qualify for course waivers or substitutions in required subjects that an ADHD/LD student is not able to pass?*

Many students with ADHD/LD find that their learning challenges make them unable to earn a passing grade in a particular required subject, despite very strong efforts to do so. Typically these tend to be math and foreign language courses that require a high level of attention to detail, consistent effort, and strong memory. Some colleges are quite accommodating when it is clear that a student has made a good-faith effort to fulfill such requirements; these institutions will allow a student to make course substitutions.

For example, a college might allow you to take a course in logic in place of a math course or a course in sign language in place of a foreign language requirement.

Other schools may require students to fail a particular course before requesting a course waiver or substitution. This can be problematic, especially if the failing grade remains part of a student's academic record.

FACULTY ATTITUDE

Is there a faculty education program to familiarize the faculty with the needs of students with ADHD or LD?

Many faculty members have limited knowledge of ADHD/LD issues, leaving them skeptical about accommodations. A faculty education program can help professors better understand brain differences and learning challenges. It can help them become more supportive of students who need accommodations.

Does the school help students identify faculty members who are particularly knowledgeable about and sympathetic toward ADHD and LD issues?

Because of training, temperament, or personal experience, some faculty members are better equipped to teach students with special learning needs. It can be extremely helpful if you know of such faculty members so that you can register for their classes.

FINDING ADHD/LD-FRIENDLY COLLEGES

A college is considered "ADHD/LD-friendly" if it is structured or focused in ways that help students with ADHD or LD function at their best. Not all students with ADHD or LD have the same needs, but certain general factors typically make a college more ADHD/LD-friendly.

When you go away to college, you're leaving lots of structure and support behind. Your chances for academic success will be greater if the college where you're heading can provide some structure and support for you while you're learning the skills to manage your ADHD independent of home and family.

SMALL SCHOOLS

S ome schools advertise a clear commitment to teaching. In many larger universities, by contrast, classes are taught by assistant professors or graduate students while more experienced faculty members focus on writing and research. There are good teachers at large universities, but as a general rule, teaching is the primary mission for faculties of smaller schools.

For many ADHD/LD students, choosing a small school over a large university is recommended. There is always the option of transferring to a larger university later—when upper level courses are typically smaller and have more personalized teaching.

SMALL CLASSES

general rule in choosing an ADHD/LD-friendly college is to look for schools with small classes. Because the classes offered to freshmen and sophomores at most state universities are large and impersonal, it may be advisable for some students to attend a small private school or a local community college during their first two years of school. Then students can transfer to a large university in their junior year to complete their studies.

However, even in a large university, once you have met the general college requirements during your freshman and sophomore years, your classes will be smaller in upper-level courses.

ACTIVE STUDENT PARTICIPATION

tudents with ADHD/LD do much better in classes whose teachers are stimulating, well-organized, and draw students into active class participation. Typically, schools with smaller class size provide such a learning environment and offer more opportunity for students to participate actively in class.

Another way to actively engage in learning is to apply what you're learning in a hands-on fashion. Some schools offer internship experience, field or independent study, mentoring, and work-study programs. Programs such as these can provide great opportunities for some ADHD and LD students and are worth looking into.

School policy at many colleges may prevent a student from requesting changes to degree requirements and core coursework. This inflexibility can make it difficult for students with specific learning challenges related to ADHD or LD. But by doing some strategic planning and making a careful selection of colleges, you can save a great deal of struggle in earning your degree.

Let's take a look at some of the most common core requirements and what you can do.

Math requirements

If math is an area of weakness for you, carefully investigate the math requirements of the schools to which you may apply. Some schools have no general math requirement. Others are flexible about course substitutions, for example, allowing a student to take a course in logic as a substitute for math. Still others have only a minimal math requirement. Additionally, it may be possible to take math during summer school or arrange for individual tutoring to help you pass the course.

Foreign language requirements

If foreign languages are difficult for you, examine each school's policy regarding foreign languages. Some schools are more flexible than others. If you doubt you will be able to pass two or more years of foreign language, explore whether the school will allow substitution of a foreign culture course or a foreign literature course taught in translation.

Another possibility, in some colleges, is to substitute a sign language course for a foreign language course. Some students are better kinesthetic (hands-on) learners than auditory learners; they find that they can master sign language much more readily than a foreign language.

If you are a stronger auditory learner than a visual learner, an intensive foreign language immersion program, where spoken language is emphasized over written language, may better suit your learning style. Ask if the school you are considering offers an immersion program or would accept credits earned in an immersion program offered by another school.

Senior thesis or senior project requirement

A senior thesis or project can become a stumbling block for students with ADHD or LD, even when they have been able to complete all other undergraduate requirements. Not all schools expect a senior thesis or senior project, but many highly competitive schools do. Certain courses of study may require senior projects.

If you decide to attend a school that requires a senior thesis or senior project, or you elect to do a thesis or research project in order to graduate with honors, you will need to carefully select your project topic and your thesis supervisor. A tutor may be able to guide you in selecting a topic or project. It will also be critical to select a thesis supervisor who you know will offer adequate structure and guidance. Additionally, you may hire a tutor to assist you specifically through each step of this challenging long-term task.

PRIORITIZING NEEDS AND PREFERENCES

Each student's needs and preferences are unique. You may not find a perfect match, but you should be able to determine very good matches and then decide which is the best choice for you. Because there are so many factors to consider when choosing a college, it's important to rank your needs and preferences in terms of priority. Along with your ADHD/LD issues to consider, choosing a college involves the careful consideration of other factors. These may include such things as expense, location, majors offered, extracurricular activities, work-study programs, and part-time attendance.

Start by making a list of things that you are seeking in a college. Then sort these things into the following categories:

- **ESSENTIAL:** These needs are so important that you will not apply to a school that cannot meet them.

- **IMPORTANT:** These needs are important to you; if a school meets most but not all of your IMPORTANT needs, you should still consider applying, so long as it can meet all of your ESSENTIAL needs.

- **DESIRABLE:** These are preferences rather than needs. Of course, you would like to attend a school that can meet your preferences as well as your needs. However, preferences rank lower on your list, after ESSENTIAL and IMPORTANT needs.

To make a list of your needs and preferences, it may be helpful to complete the following questionnaire. Discuss your answers with your parents and perhaps a teacher or school counselor who knows you well so that you don't overlook any important or essential needs.

This questionnaire has been developed to help you think about a broad range of considerations and then prioritize them. These are only some of the many things you will need to consider when choosing a college, but this list highlights the primary issues you'll need to think about.

COLLEGE PREFERENCES QUESTIONNAIRE

STEP 1 - SELECT ATTRIBUTES

Your first step is to check all the items below that describe what you are seeking in a college or university.

Physical/geographical considerations

❑ Close to home

❑ Located in a particular region of the country

❑ Small student body

❑ Medium-sized student body

❑ Large student body

❑ Urban setting

❑ Suburban setting

❑ Rural setting

Housing considerations

❑ On-campus housing available for freshmen and sophomores

❑ Provision of a private or single-occupancy dorm room

❑ Specialized dorms such as

    ❑ Quiet dorms or halls

    ❑ Nonsmoking dorms or halls

    ❑ Foreign-language-focused dorms or halls

Financial considerations

❑ Charges in-state tuition rates

❑ Offers scholarship money

❑ Close enough to commute from home (to avoid housing costs)

❑ Offers work-study options

Religious considerations

❑ Is affiliated with my family's religion

❑ Has a religious affiliation

❑ Has no religious affiliation

Athletic interests

❑ Offers the opportunity to play a competitive sport

❑ Recruits me to play a competitive sport

❑ Provides an opportunity to play intramural sports

❑ Provides the opportunity to pursue a more individual athletic interest (skiing, horseback riding, fencing)

Artistic interests

❑ Offers high-level training in an area of artistic skill such as drama, music, or art

❑ Provides a broad range of art, music, and theater courses for non-majors

❑ Has a lively arts or music scene

Social considerations

❑ Has active fraternities and sororities

❑ Has a diverse student body

❑ Has a socially/politically conservative student body

❑ Has a socially/politically liberal student body

❑ Is attended by one or more of my friends

Type of college

❑ A two-year college from which I can later transfer to a four-year college

❑ A four-year college where I can remain throughout my undergraduate education

❑ A university with both undergraduate and graduate programs

Other academic considerations

❑ Academically competitive

❑ Provides a strong program in my area of interest

❑ Has small classes and a strong emphasis on teaching

❑ Offers a broad range of academic majors

❑ Offers a range of practical/career-focused majors

❑ Has a strong study-abroad program

Work/career considerations

❑ Offers an active work-study program

❑ Emphasizes internships offering work experience

STEP 2 - CATEGORIZE CONSIDERATIONS

Now, list those items you have checked in Step 1 under one of the three categories below: Essential, Important, or Desirable.

If you're like many students, this part of the task may be the most difficult for you. Everything you've checked may seem essential. It may help to sit down with a friend, parent, or counselor to discuss the checked items and place them in prioritized categories. If possible, place five or fewer items in the Essential category. Remember, "essential" means you won't apply to a school unless it offers all these items.

Essential
I won't attend a college unless it offers all of the following:

1. _____
2. _____
3. _____
4. _____
5. _____

Important
It's important but not critical that a college offers the following:

1. _____
2. _____
3. _____
4. _____
5. _____

Desirable

These things are desirable but are not determining factors in my college selection.

1. _____
2. _____
3. _____
4. _____
5. _____

Think about your list for a week or so, allowing yourself to move items in and out of categories until you are clear in your mind which characteristics a school must have, which characteristics are important to you, and which characteristics are desirable but you can live without.

STEP 3 - RANK CONSIDERATIONS

Now, rank your Important items in order of priority. It's likely that no school will be a perfect match, so you need to be aware which items here are *most* important. That way you can focus more on them as you begin your college search.

You and your parents may disagree on what is Essential, Important, and Desirable. If there are several areas of disagreement, it may be useful for your parents to complete a questionnaire listing their own preferences. You can then compare notes. If you and your parents cannot reach agreement through talking at home, it may be helpful to discuss this questionnaire with your school counselor or a college advisor.

CREATING A LIST OF COLLEGES

Now that you have your list of Essential, Important, and Desirable items, it's time to start looking for schools that will be a good match. As you begin, focus first on colleges that meet *all* Essential items (remember if it's essential, you won't attend without it) and those Important items near the top of your list.

There are many sources of information to help you find colleges that meet your requirements:

- SCHOOL COUNSELORS: Often the best place to begin is by speaking with an academic advisor or college counselor at your high school.

- INTERNET SEARCHES: Up-to-date information can often be found by doing Internet searches. For example, if you search the Internet for "small liberal arts colleges," "college interior design program," or "college ecology major," you will find a broad range of information at your fingertips.

- COLLEGE GUIDES: Numerous college guides, updated annually, provide a great deal of general information. Such guides can be found in your local bookstore or high school library.

- **COLLEGES AND UNIVERSITIES:** Contacting colleges directly via the Internet, by phone, or in person is a great way to gather information.

- **SPECIALIZED PRIVATE COLLEGE COUNSELOR:** As colleges and universities provide more supports for ADHD or LD, private college counselors have come to specialize in guiding students with specific learning needs. Although this service can be relatively costly, it may be a good investment.

APPLYING TO COLLEGE

The college application process generally begins in your junior year of high school as you prepare to take the SATs and ends a year later as you mail off your applications. Most college counselors advise applying to at least one school as a "safety"— namely one that you are sure will accept you. You should also apply to several colleges that are likely to accept you, and to one or two "reach" colleges that you hope will accept you.

Here are some steps in the college application process:

1   Prepare to take the SATs. Should you take SAT prep classes or work with a private tutor? Many students with ADHD or LD find that they work best in a one-on-one situation with a tutor who can help them identify subject matter they will need extra help with. Tutors can provide tips on test-taking that are customized to your particular learning style.

2   Take the SATs. It's recommended to schedule the SAT early in the school year so that you can take it more than once, if you are not satisfied with your initial scores.

3   Create your college list, based on needs and preferences (Essential, Important, or Desirable). As you gather information, work to pare down your list to schools you will realistically consider. It may be helpful to work on your list with your school counselor, a private college counselor, or both.

4   Visit colleges. A good time to start your college visits is during spring break of your junior year. If possible, visit while classes are in session. It's a good idea to visit every school to which you plan to apply. You may find that after visiting a school, it moves higher up your list or drops off it altogether.

5   Write your college essays. You may benefit from working with a tutor who can help you structure and develop your essay(s). The tutor can give you important pointers on how to strengthen your essay and get it into the best possible shape.

6   Request letters of recommendation. Give your letter writers plenty of time to complete this task. It is useful to discuss with them pertinent and supporting information (your interests, ambitions, strengths, etc.) as well as why a particular school or program would be a good match for you. This will assist them in writing a strong letter of reference.

7   Complete and mail your applications.

8   Inform your high school counselor and the Educational Testing Service (which administers the SAT) where to send your grades and scores.

9   Follow up with each school to make sure it has received all the materials needed to complete your application.

CHAPTER SUMMARY

• • • Choosing the right college takes time. Get started early in your junior year and plan to visit colleges during your spring break.

• • • Get all the help you need in creating your college list. Help may come from school counselors, your parents, college guides, or a private specialized college counselor.

• • • Be sure that you understand how you are affected by ADHD/LD and what accommodations and supports you'll need in college to succeed.

• • • Take the time to make sure each college you consider has the support services you'll need.

• • • Look for ADHD/LD-friendly colleges.

• • • Take the college application process step-by-step, getting support and assistance along the way.

CHAPTER 2

HELP ON CAMPUS

This chapter focuses on how to take full advantage of the supports and services available to you once you arrive on campus. There are many supports and privileges provided that are designed to help you perform to your full potential. However, it is your responsibility to take advantage of those supports. The best approach is to build collaborative relationships with all of your counselors, advisors, and professors, taking steps that allow them to get to know you and your specific learning challenges.

Even if you prefer not to take advantage of accommodations that you are eligible for, it is a good idea to develop a relationship with your support services advisor and your professors to make them aware of your learning challenges. It's perfectly acceptable to inform your professors of your eligibility for accommodations while also telling them that you would prefer to wait to see if you will need them.

Informing your professors in advance will earn their respect for your decision to wait and see. In addition, they will not think you're simply making excuses if you later ask for accommodations if you experience difficulty in their class.

USING SUPPORT SERVICES
OR ACCOMMODATIONS IN COLLEGE

Many high school students are eager to leave their ADHD or LD labels behind as they head for college, shedding an old identity as a student with ADHD or LD and making a fresh start in a new place. Other students, because they have received few accommodations in high school, don't believe that any supports will be necessary during college.

It's important to understand that college differs from high school in many ways. For example, many students feel stigmatized during their earlier school years if they are placed in special support classes. In college, however, learning supports are typically provided in an independent and private fashion. If anything, other students who are aware of your accommodations will view them as a privilege rather than something to feel ashamed of.

College differs in other important ways as well. Even if you've been able to get through high school without supports or accommodations, this doesn't necessarily mean you won't need them in college. College reading and writing assignments are usually more demanding than those in high school.

You will also be expected to function much more independently, without the same level of support from parents and teachers that you had in high school. Managing your time, your assignments, and your daily life activities often poses a greater challenge than do academic requirements for many students with ADHD.

Even if you do not plan to use ADHD or LD support services, you will be at a great advantage by attending a school where such services are available. Later, if you find that you are experiencing academic difficulties, ADHD or LD services will be there waiting for you. A faculty fully aware of the needs of ADHD or LD students is attuned to students with different learning styles and needs. Such a faculty is often willing to be more flexible in its requirements.

DEVELOPING A RELATIONSHIP WITH THE STUDENT SUPPORT SERVICES OFFICE

Make your first contact with the student support services office at the time of your initial campus visit (before you apply to that college and are accepted by it). It can also be helpful to talk to other students on campus who receive support services. Sometimes these interactions can take place informally, by talking to students who may be visiting the support center at the time of your visit. Otherwise, ask if there is a student who would be willing to talk to you.

It is your choice whether to disclose that you have learning or attentional problems when you make your college application. Once you have been accepted at a college and have decided to attend it, it is a good idea to telephone the student support services office. Let them know you will be a student at their school and send them a copy of your most recent test report.

Once you arrive on campus, make an appointment with the student support services office within the first few days. Your goal should be to present yourself as a motivated student who understands your strengths and weaknesses and wants to function at your best during college. In this first appointment, reexamine the range of services available on campus and determine with your support services counselor, what accommodations you will need.

Some of the first questions to ask include:

- When should I let my professors know that I have ADHD or LD? When do I request accommodations?

- How do I inform professors of my need for accommodations? Will your office provide me with an official letter outlining the accommodations that I qualify for?

- Who is my academic advisor? Does this individual have any experience in working with ADHD or LD students? If not, may I come to the student support services office for assistance in selecting my classes?

- Is there an ADHD or LD student support group on campus that I can join?

- May I make regular appointments with you during my first term on campus?

- Is there a physician on campus who can prescribe stimulant medication for me (if you are a student who takes stimulant medication for ADHD)? How do I make an appointment with this person?

QUALIFYING FOR ADHD OR LD ACCOMMODATIONS

An "accommodation" is a change in procedure specifically designed to assist a student with learning differences to be able to perform at his or her best. Common accommodations for students with ADHD or LD include:

- Extended time when taking quizzes, tests, and exams.

- Opportunity to take a quiz, test, or exam in a quiet, nondistracting environment.

- Opportunity to take a quiz, test, or exam on a computer.

- Opportunity to have a note-taker in each class, permission to tape each class, or access to the professor's notes for each class.

- Early registration privileges to allow you to custom-design your class schedule.

To qualify for accommodations, you must have up-to-date documentation of a disability (in the form of a complete psychoeducational or neuropsychological test battery). Most colleges require documentation that is less than three years old. If you received accommodations in high school, you will not automatically qualify for them in college. Most colleges require a recent set of tests that clearly demonstrate areas of disability, along with a test report that recommends specific accommodations.

Carefully review with your college support services advisor the recommendations made in your test report. Make sure the report clearly recommends accommodations. In some cases, the student support services office will require more information from the person who wrote your report before they will approve the recommended accommodations.

If your most recent test report is out of date, some colleges will temporarily accommodate you while you and your parents arrange for current testing. Such testing is the responsibility of the student and his or her family. The college does not typically provide it.

REQUESTING ACCOMMODATIONS

Asking for accommodations is not asking for a favor. Accommodations justified by your test documentation are your legal right. Students' rights are protected under the Rehabilitation Act (RA) of 1973 and the Americans with Disabilities Act (ADA), which bar discrimination, and by the Individuals with Disabilities Education Act (IDEA), which mandates free, appropriate education at the primary and secondary levels. Combining the RA with the IDEA extends this mandate to the college level.

Schools are not required by law to change their admission standards or requirements for graduation. Schools are required to provide accommodations for your ADHD or LD so that you can have the most successful and enjoyable college experience possible. It's best to request accommodations and have them in place, even if you believe you won't need them. That way, if you begin to experience academic difficulties, the mechanism is already established to provide assistance.

You can use your own judgment about whether or not to take advantage of an accommodation in a specific situation. For example, you might complete multiple-choice tests fairly rapidly and not need extended time on such a test. On the other hand, you may find that you need more time when answering essay questions.

Once you have established yourself as a student who is eligible for extended time on tests, you can use this accommodation selectively, when you feel you need it.

SELECTING CLASSES

Before school begins, work with your academic advisor to select your classes. Ideally, your support services advisor will also be your academic advisor. That way, the person who knows your learning needs best will be advising you when you register for classes. Your advisor can help guide you toward professors who are knowledgeable about, and supportive of, students with ADHD or LD. In many schools, however, your academic advisor will not be a specialist in ADHD or LD. If your official academic advisor is not a learning specialist, ask whether your support services advisor can guide you as you make your course selections.

In addition to talking to your advisor, invest time in talking to other students and in learning which are the best and most ADHD/LD-friendly teachers and courses for you. You may also wish to talk to professors about their knowledge of ADHD or LD, and whether they would accommodate your requests for different or alternative tests, quizzes, and assignments.

Careful planning and advising will help you develop a well-thought-out class schedule each term. Below, you'll find a list of factors to take into account in developing your class schedule each term.

- Avoid registering for several courses with heavy reading or writing requirements during the same term. You can typically determine reading or writing workload by looking at a syllabus or contacting the professor. Syllabi are often available online.

- Balance your schedule each term. For example, if you are a slow reader, try to limit yourself to no more than two classes with heavy reading requirements per term. If you anticipate that certain required courses will be especially demanding, buffer your course load with less demanding elective classes. Additionally, try to mix your most interesting classes with required courses that may interest you less.

- Consider registering for more classes than you plan to take. This allows you to use the "drop and add" period after classes begin to strategically drop classes that prove to be a poor match for you.

- Carefully review the syllabus of each course after the first class. Evaluate whether the reading and writing assignments are possible for you to fulfill, given your other course work.

- Take a reduced course load. For example, take 12 course hours when 15 or 16 is a standard load. Most students with ADHD or LD function much better by taking fewer courses. A reduced course load each term will mean that you will need to take courses during summer school, or plan to take an extra semester or two to graduate. While it may not sound appealing to stretch out your studies, requiring more time to graduate, you'll be much better off earning good grades each term.

- If possible, avoid successive classes during the day without a break or classes that meet for longer than one hour.

- Choose classes that fit your schedule, but be realistic about yourself. For example, if you have great difficulty getting up in the morning, try to arrange a class schedule that begins after 10:00 a.m.

- During some terms, you may have to take classes at inconvenient times. When this is the case, develop strategies, perhaps by working with an ADHD coach, to make sure you don't sabotage yourself through poor class attendance.

- Avoid large lectures if at all possible. Small classes with group discussion will enhance your comprehension and concentration.

- Ask your support services advisor if he or she can recommend particular professors who work well with students with ADHD or LD. Not all advisors will have such information, but many will. Ask other students this question too. On a number of campuses, students with ADHD or LD create their own list of recommended professors. Whenever possible, select courses taught by these professors.

REGISTERING FOR COURSES

Many schools allow students with ADHD or LD early registration each term to provide better access to the courses and professors they need. This is an increasingly common privilege for students with ADHD/LD and one that you should take full advantage of. Even with careful academic advising, the best-laid plans will go awry if you find that the courses you've been advised to take, or the particular professors you've been advised to select, are no longer available.

Using early registration, you'll be better able to customize your schedule to meet your needs. Consider registering for more classes than you plan to take. This allows you to drop some of your classes without having to change the rest of your schedule.

DEVELOPING GOOD WORKING RELATIONSHIPS WITH YOUR PROFESSORS

Some professors are supportive and understanding, either because they have background or training in the field, or because they have a personal knowledge or experience with ADHD or LD. However, a number of professors may be resistant to, or skeptical about, accommodating students with ADHD or LD. Many do not understand learning differences and why accommodations are reasonable or necessary. In any case, you can do a lot to develop a good relationship with your professors and demonstrate your hard work and commitment to academic success.

Your best approach to building a positive, supportive relationship with your professors is to contact each of them individually during the first week of class and make an appointment to meet with them during their office hours. (It will help you be organized if you write each professor's office hours down in a single list. Use those office hours regularly.)

During your first meeting with your professor, discuss with him or her your written statement (typically provided by student support services office) that documents your eligibility for accommodations and outlines your particular needs. Your goal in this meeting, and in later meetings with your professors, is to establish that you are a highly motivated student with specific learning needs.

Be prepared to discuss your situation beyond what is provided on the written statement. (You might even practice talking about this with your advisor or parent.) In doing so, you will help your professor better understand your learning challenges. Here are some things you might consider discussing with your professors:

- If you have a written language disability, explain what this means to your professor. Ask if he or she would consider not discounting your grade for spelling and punctuation errors on in-class writing assignments where you cannot check your spelling or punctuation.

- Alternatively, ask your professor that you be allowed to write on your computer, even for informal, in-class quizzes and assignments.

- If you have significant problems putting your thoughts in writing, ask your professor if he or she would be willing to give you a private verbal exam following your written exam. Explain that this would give you an opportunity to demonstrate your knowledge in a format that is a greater strength for you.

- If you have significant memory-retrieval problems, explain your difficulties at the beginning of the term. Some professors may be willing to provide you with tests or quizzes in a format that will allow you to better demonstrate your knowledge. For example, some students experience great difficulty with multiple-choice questions or fill-in-the-blank questions, but can demonstrate their knowledge if allowed to write short essays or take verbal exams. Another option is to request a take-home exam.

- If you tend to do poorly on exams, even when you've studied hard, ask the professor if he or she would consider accepting extra-credit work in order to compensate for lower test scores.

A professor is not obliged to provide these accommodations. However, if you establish yourself as a hard-working, motivated student and have explained your learning challenges in advance, a professor is much more likely to be flexible in working with you. When you have established a positive relationship with your professor—by attending class regularly, by participating in class, and by making regular appointments to discuss any problems you may be experiencing in the course—your professor will be much more likely to make informal accommodations for you.

Most students who take a positive approach and demonstrate their motivation find that a majority of professors are responsive and encouraging. If, however, a particular professor or instructor does not respond in a positive manner to your request for accommodations, consider switching to another class or section during the "drop and add" period of the term, generally the first two weeks of each term.

TAKING ADVANTAGE OF
OTHER ACADEMIC SUPPORTS ON CAMPUS

During grade school and high school, most students with ADHD or LD benefit from the structure and support provided by their parents, as well as by their counselors, coaches, and tutors. In college, the responsibility lies with the student to seek out and take advantage of support services on campus.

Often, a student who is not accustomed to initiating contact with support services will wait far too long to seek them out, resulting sometimes in low or even failing grades. A better approach as you enter college is to take advantage of all available support. Then, as you gain a better sense of the demands of college, you can eliminate supports that don't seem necessary or helpful.

In addition to specific ADHD/LD supports, most college campuses offer academic supports that are available to all students. These might include:

- **PEER TUTORING:** tutoring provided by students who have a strong knowledge base in a particular subject area.

- **WRITING LAB:** a place on campus, open to all, where students can obtain guidance and assistance in completing writing assignments. Often a writing lab is staffed by upperclassmen or graduate students.

- **LANGUAGE LAB:** a campus service where students can hone their foreign language skills by listening to audiotapes.

During the first two years, most of your classes will be chosen to meet your core graduation requirements, the classes that all students must take to earn a degree. At some point during your sophomore year (if not earlier), it is time to think about and select a major, the area of study that will become the primary focus of your last two years of college.

Although some students have a clear area of interest as they enter college, many college students begin with little notion of what they want to study. It is not unusual for students to change their selection of a major at least once. Sometimes an area of study turns out to be less appealing than a student had anticipated. In other instances, a change of major is sparked by an interesting summer job or an appealing professor who makes a particular subject come alive.

The selection of a college major is an important decision for all students, but it is especially so for those with ADHD or LD. Students with special learning challenges will have a greater chance for success in college when they pursue an area of strong interest. This allows them to focus on their strengths while also taking areas of weakness into account.

In order to make a good choice, it can be helpful to list all your strengths. Many students with ADHD or LD are more aware of their learning difficulties than of their personal and academic strengths.

Write a list of stengths. For example, such a list might include:

- ☐ Good with people
- ☐ Love to talk
- ☐ Lots of energy
- ☐ Determination
- ☐ Good problem-solver
- ☐ Lots of ideas
- ☐ Verbal expression
- ☐ Good writer/writing skills
- ☐ Good reading skills
- ☐ Good reasoning ability
- ☐ Artistic

Then write a list of difficulties. These might include, for example:

- ☐ Tend to overlook details
- ☐ Dislike paperwork
- ☐ Absent-minded
- ☐ Difficulty with science
- ☐ Difficulty with math
- ☐ Memory problems

Go over these lists with your advisor to receive assistance in making a good match among your strengths, weaknesses, and the academic requirements in each major. Another rich source of information about your strengths and weaknesses can be found in your ADHD/LD test report.

You should also consider probable job requirements after college, as well as whether you will need graduate training in your chosen field.

Don't let your areas of difficulty completely dictate your choice! If you have a burning desire to study a particular subject, by all means pursue that interest! Your extra motivation can help you overcome the obstacles presented by your learning problems. And as you well know, your own hard work, combined with the support services available, can help you succeed.

EXPLORING WORK-STUDY EXPERIENCES AND INTERNSHIPS

Often one of the best ways to test out a career that you are considering is to gain hands-on experience in the field. Some schools offer excellent opportunities to engage in work-study programs that can even allow you to earn course credits.

Most schools try to help students arrange for internship experiences, either during the academic year or over the summer. Check with your support services provider to find out what office on campus assists students in applying for internships.

Start early since the best internships go fast! This is your chance to try on a job, making it worth the extra effort of seeking out interesting internship opportunities.

SEEKING CAREER COUNSELING

Specialized career counseling can be particularly helpful for the ADHD or LD student. Such counseling ideally should involve ability testing in addition to testing to assess attentional or learning problems. Personality testing can sometimes be helpful. Interest testing is also very important. Assessments may include:

- **INTEREST INVENTORY:** A lengthy questionnaire that asks you to indicate your level of interest in a broad range of topics and activities. Interest inventories, available through your college counseling center, can help you think in a more organized manner about your interests and the types of jobs that relate to your interests. Such inventories are typically computer-scored; they match your expressed interests against people who have been successful in many different kinds of work. The inventory results won't tell you if you have the skills needed to succeed in a particular career, but they will tell you which careers align with your interests.

- **PERSONALITY TESTING:** Several personality tests have been used in connection with career counseling. In addition, research has been conducted on which personality types seem to be good matches for certain careers. Personality tests are often available at your campus counseling center.

- **ABILITY TESTS:** Many students with ADHD or LD become overly focused on their disability, leading them to ignore or overlook their own special abilities. A number of ability tests are available today. Some may be offered through your career counseling office; others can be privately pursued. A good ability-test battery will analyze clusters of natural ability; it can then direct you toward career paths that will maximize those innate strengths.

After completing career testing, don't expect to be given one or two specific career choices. The purpose of career testing is to help identify broad areas of interest that may match to a variety of careers. From this, your career counselor will talk to you about general areas of ability and interest, and will help guide you toward a choice within these areas.

Some students with ADHD or LD approach the selection of their major from a negative standpoint: "Let's see, I'm not good in math, so I shouldn't take science courses." Or, "I'm a slow reader, so I shouldn't take anything in the humanities." Students who make their choices through a process of elimination may find themselves in a field that doesn't really interest them.

Instead of emphasizing your weaknesses, focus on your strengths and interests, then problem-solve to work around areas of difficulty. For example: "What I'd really like to do is go into business. I know that I have difficulty with math, and that math is required to earn a business degree. Let me talk to my advisor and to someone in the business school to explore my options. Maybe some course substitutions would be allowed, or I'll be able to handle the math courses with the help of a tutor. Maybe some areas of business emphasize math less than others."

The key to a positive career choice is to follow your heart's desire while being realistic about your strengths and challenges.

CHAPTER SUMMARY

• • • Develop a relationship with counselors at the student support services center. You'll get much more out of their services if they know you well and understand your particular needs.

• • • Develop a close working relationship with each of your professors. Make sure they know your needs and know that you are a motivated student who will work hard to succeed but may need accommodations.

• • • Select your courses carefully each term, with the guidance of an ADHD/LD specialist, if possible.

• • • Select your major and your career direction carefully, taking your needs, strengths, and interests into account. It may be very helpful to work with a career counselor who understands ADHD/LD during this process.

CHAPTER 3

HELP IN THE COMMUNITY

Although many services and supports are available on most college campuses, you may find that you need to supplement those services by seeking private services in your college community.

HIRING A PRIVATE TUTOR

While peer tutoring may be available on campus, you may need more intensive, specialized tutoring in a particular subject. Often the academic support center keeps a list of private tutors in the community who can tutor you for an hourly fee. This is a costly alternative, but it may be a good investment.

A private tutor can work with you to improve your general study skills so that you can prepare more effectively for exams. A tutor can also help you become better at selecting the most critical information in long reading assignments, and help you learn to write papers and reports more efficiently.

Tutoring should also focus on planning, organization, and study skills, as well as on your specific areas of difficulty. If your learning disabilities involve both language skills and math, you may need different tutors for each area.

FINDING MEDICAL CONSULTATION

Some colleges have a contract with a local psychiatrist who visits the student health services office on a regular basis to prescribe stimulant medication or other medications for related conditions such as anxiety or depression.

If this service is not available, or if a student needs more intensive or specialized care, often the learning support center or student health center on campus can provide names of physicians in the community who are experienced in treating college students with ADHD. You should also ask your physician at home if he or she can make a referral to anyone in your college community. Other sources of information about professionals with expertise in working with students with ADHD or LD can be found by an Internet search.

Follow-up care is essential to good treatment for ADHD. Obtaining prescriptions for ADHD medication can be complicated, but it is becoming increasingly common and more manageable for college students. Because these prescriptions are for controlled substances, they cannot be phoned into a pharmacy, and out-of-state prescriptions will not be honored. For these reasons, you should find a physician in your college town who can work with you.

USING COUNSELING OR PSYCHOTHERAPY

Psychotherapy can be very helpful for students dealing with issues such as anxiety, stress, homesickness, or problems with self-esteem and interpersonal relationships. Such difficulties should not be ignored. To succeed in college, you will need to focus your energy on academic pursuits. If you are struggling with emotional troubles, self-doubts, loneliness, or social isolation, your academic tasks may become unmanageable. Don't wait until you are in a crisis to seek help.

Your college counseling service can be a good place to start. However, if you find that it offers only short-term help, ask for a referral to a mental health professional in the community who has experience working with students who have learning or attention difficulties.

You may need support, advice, and counseling as you make the transition to independent college living. Many young adults do. A complete treatment program for ADHD involves not only medication, but also counseling to learn to make realistic decisions, to understand your ADHD better, and to learn mechanisms to cope with the stress and frustration that often accompany ADHD.

As you may imagine, college (with its new stresses) may be a good time to reenter therapy. It is a good idea to have the names of a couple of professionals on campus or in your college community whom you can contact if the need arises.

WORKING WITH AN ADHD COACH

Many students with ADHD or LD can feel overwhelmed in college without the structure and support they had when living at home. They may struggle with irregular sleep habits, forgetfulness, difficulty budgeting money, and problems managing their time. They may have trouble balancing academics, social life, daily life management tasks, and healthy daily habits.

ADHD coaching can be an effective way to help you learn to better manage your daily life. Coaching focuses on improving time management, learning to set and reach goals, learning to build better habits, and developing the skills needed to meet the demands of daily life. Coaching is an ideal support for students needing help with these challenges.

College academic support services rarely provide ADHD coaching. You will most likely need to seek it out privately. Unlike physicians, tutors, or psychotherapists, an ADHD coach doesn't necessarily need to be located directly in your college community (the coaching can take place via phone and Internet). Often an ADHD coach may work with students spread out across a large geographic range.

CHAPTER SUMMARY

• • • All of the supports you need may not be available on campus. You may need to seek help from private professionals in your college community.

• • • Your student support services office may be able to recommend psychiatrists, psychotherapists, tutors, and ADHD coaches experienced in working with college students.

CHAPTER 4

WAYS TO HELP YOURSELF

The preceding chapters have focused on making a college choice that is a good match and on finding support and accommodations both on campus and through professionals in the community. Now, in this chapter, the focus is on the most critical success factor of all: taking charge of your ADHD or LD challenges and developing the learning and organization strategies that will allow you to do your best academically.

The strategies and habits discussed in this chapter will require effort and persistence to develop. Although some students with ADHD or LD may have already developed good organizing and study habits, other students may find that they have difficulty being consistent in following the suggestions you'll read in this chapter. If this is true for you, don't get discouraged, get help!

Individuals with learning challenges who become successful in their careers almost universally report that the support and encouragement of others was key to their success.

There are numerous sources of support that you may find useful, including:

- Meeting regularly with your academic support services advisor as you work to develop better study habits.

- Working with a specialized ADHD or LD tutor.

- Working with an ADHD coach.

- Joining a student support group on campus.

- Joining or forming a study group on campus.

As you begin to develop consistent planning, organization, and study habits, you may gradually need less support from others. But as you're getting started, make sure that you seek out all the support you need to succeed.

MANAGING YOUR TIME

In college you have more unstructured time than you had in high school, and probably more than you will have after you enter the professional world. Many students, unaccustomed to so much free time, don't plan their day well. With lots of unstructured time, it's easy to believe that there's plenty of time to do it later. Unfortunately, many students fall into this time-management trap and find themselves pulling all-nighters and turning in assignments at the last minute, or even late.

Although most college students have difficulty managing their time well, it is especially challenging for students with ADHD to develop good time-management habits. As you learn to use an electronic or paper planner to outline the activities of your days and weeks, you'll soon realize that all of that free time when you're not in class will fill up quickly with studying as well as planned activities.

USING DAY PLANNERS, CALENDARS, AND LISTS

If you are unaccustomed to using a day planner, you may want to experiment with several systems before you find one that works for you.

Planners come in both paper and electronic forms. Most college students prefer a portable electronic organizer, such as a PDA (personal digital assistant), which can be synched with a planner on your laptop or desktop computer.

Some students prefer to use a paper planner. Some students use computer calendars (with reminder functions). Others like creating detailed to-do lists. There are even planner systems that let you use both, that is, a computer-based electronic planner from which pages can be printed and carried in a specially designed notebook.

Whether you use a paper or electronic format, select a system that is convenient to keep with you throughout the day and easy to use.

MANAGING DAY-TO-DAY SCHEDULES

All of your activities and commitments should be written in your day planner (or other organizing system), with the times blocked out. Be sure to include time for meals, travel time to and from classes, class time, chores such as laundry and errands, sports or other campus activities, appointments, and social life as well as time to complete your academic assignments. On the next page is an example of how a typical day in a college student's day planner might look. In addition, here are a few time-management tips to consider:

- Set aside 10 to 15 minutes daily to plan and map out your day.

- Try not to overbook yourself and don't forget to block out time for relaxation! You will need it, and you will take it whether it is scheduled or not.

- As you block out study time, be realistic. You will need frequent study breaks in order to maintain concentration and focus, and ample time to enjoy your academic work.

- Use time on campus between classes as study time. Although it is tempting to take a break, you will probably find that you get more done by studying in hour-long segments interspersed throughout the day. Many college students plan to study for several hours in the evening, but find that they are tired (or distracted by other students) and unable to get much studying done.

- Make sure you plan enough time to get adequate sleep. Try to allow at least eight hours between lights out and your first class the following day. Many students fall into the night-owl trap, creating a situation in which they are chronically sleep-deprived and unable to follow their planned daily schedule.

✔	TO DO:	HOUR	SCHEDULE
		7:00	
		7:30	
✓	LAUNDRY	8:00	BREAKFAST
		8:30	
✓	Library	9:00	Start laundry
	get references	9:30	
	for paper	10:00	Chemistry
		10:30	
		11:00	Library
		11:30	
		NOON	LUNCH
✓	Call Lisa	12:30	
		1:00	Anthropology
	make appt	1:30	
	with	2:00	Errands
	tutor	2:30	
		3:00	Chemistry Lab
		3:30	
	couldn't reach	4:00	
	him — call	4:30	
	tomorrow	5:00	BREAK
		5:30	
		6:00	DINNER
		6:30	Put Laundry in dryer
		7:00	Study
		7:30	
		8:00	
		8:30	Read Anthro. Ch 3
		9:00	
		9:30	BREAK
		10:00	
		10:30	Read
		11:00	Write tomorrow's schedule
		11:30	Turn off TV!
		12:00	Bedtime

SCHEDULING PROJECTS AND ASSIGNMENTS

In high school, you may have a few long-term papers or projects, but most assignments are daily assignments given in class, to be completed in the evening and turned in the next day. In college, however, most of your assignments will be given to you at the beginning of each term in the form of a syllabus, a summary outline of a course of study. You'll receive a syllabus for each class that outlines reading assignments, papers, and exam dates for the term. It's up to you to take the information on each syllabus and translate it into a study schedule for the term.

During the first week of classes, review the syllabus from each course and record in your planner the dates of all exams, as well as the pre-assigned dates for reading and writing assignments. Divide each reading assignment into small bites. Keep in mind what works best for you.

If you are a slow reader or you sometimes lose concentration while reading, don't expect to read an entire chapter at one sitting. The more dense the reading material (that is, the more detailed the new information is in the assignment), the more time you need to devote to it. For example, you might be able to read 75 pages of a novel assigned for English class at one sitting, but you may be able to concentrate on only 10 pages of your chemistry text before you need a break. Whatever the reading assignment is, determine what you can read at one sitting. Divide the entire assignment into such manageable reading periods, and schedule each period.

If you have a 25-page paper to write or a long-term research project to complete, break the large project into a list of smaller tasks. For example:

1   Discuss possible topics with your professor.

2   Do a literature search, looking in computer databases, in the library catalog, and on the Internet for relevant articles and publications. Copy the list of references.

3   Determine with your professor how many articles you need to read. Go to the library and make copies of those articles.

4   Read, underline, and outline five or more articles on large note cards.

5   Read, underline, and outline five more articles.

6   Read, underline, and outline the remaining articles.

7   Make a list of relevant books and authors. Be sure to copy all information needed for your bibliography.

8   Take notes from the books you have selected for your paper. (If you need to, talk to your tutor about how to glean needed information from a book without having to read the entire book.)

9   Make an outline of your paper, and discuss it with your professor.

10 Write a rough draft of the paper on your computer. Don't forget to spell-check and grammar-check your draft.

11 Ask your professor or check a style manual for an appropriate form for your bibliography, and type it.

12 Take your rough draft to your tutor. Work with him or her on the organization and structure of your paper, and ways to develop and elaborate your ideas.

13 Write the final draft of your paper.

14 Take the final draft to your tutor if you need assistance with final revisions.

15 Make revisions on the computer and print your final copy.

For a research project, the process of breaking down a long-term project into daily steps is similar. For example:

1   Meet with your professor to discuss possible research topics.

2   Do database, library, and Internet searches to refine your topic.

3   Meet with your professor again to discuss your research design, determining the number of subjects you'll need in your experimental and control groups.

4   Write an initial draft of your research proposal. This should contain a review of relevant research, propose a hypothesis to test, and outline the methods by which you will test your hypothesis, including how many experimental and control subjects you plan to include in your study. Then obtain your professor's approval for your proposal.

5   Speak with your professor about other faculty members who should be involved in supervising you on your research project. For example, discuss who will assist you with your statistical analysis of data.

6   Collect your data from both experimental and control subjects.

7   Analyze your data with the supervision and assistance of a statistician.

8   Write the results and discussion sections of your research paper.

9   Submit your paper to your professor for review.

10   Make any changes required following your professor's review.

11   Print out your paper in its final form and submit it.

After you have made a task list such as the one above, your next step is to estimate how much time you will need for each task. Write the estimated time next to each task. Then go to your day planner and assign a day and time for each task. One good way to do this is to begin with the date the paper is due and work backward.

In addition to entering these bite-sized tasks into your planner, many students find it is helpful to create a time line on a large wall-sized calendar. This allows you to measure your progress with one quick glance. As you advance through your long-term project, you'll probably need to make midcourse corrections; some tasks may take longer than planned, and unexpected events may interfere with your initial plan.

DISCOVERING YOUR LEARNING STYLE

It may sound odd that we all need to "learn how to learn," but many students arrive at college without having developed good learning skills. By listening in class, doing some of the homework, and reading the material before a test, many bright students manage to do well in high school without developing good study skills. In college, however, the demands rapidly increase. Students who have learned how to read material efficiently and select the most important facts from it, students who understand their learning style and study in a way that is consistent with it, and students who have developed effective memory techniques will be at a great advantage in college.

Learn as much as you can about your best learning style. Are you an auditory learner, a visual learner, or a hands-on learner? Do you learn best while moving? Do you learn best while interacting with others, or while studying alone in a quiet, nondistracting environment?

If you're not sure of your learning style, it may help to experiment. For example, try reading part of a chapter silently, taking notes. Then tackle the second half of the chapter using an auditory approach: Read aloud to yourself, then "take notes" by talking into a tape recorder. Afterward, test yourself by making up a set of note cards asking questions about the most important facts covered by the chapter. Did you learn better as a visual learner or as an auditory learner? Many students learn best when using more than one approach, for example, listening to a recorded text while simultaneously reading that text.

Academics tend to be most challenging for hands-on learners because few scholarly subjects are taught in an experiential fashion that gives students hands-on learning opportunities. Hands-on learners are typically most successful if they are engaged in practical courses of training that allow them to build and create.

Overall, plan your study techniques in relationship to your best learning style. Auditory learners should say things aloud. Visual learners are more likely to remember what they have seen; that's why preparing notes with color highlights of essential facts can make them more memorable.

Study tips for auditory learners

- If you learn best by hearing, read aloud to yourself while studying.

- Consider forming a study group for each or most of your classes. Members of these groups can discuss class notes and study for tests by quizzing one another aloud.

- When studying alone, instead of taking notes, dictate into a handheld tape recorder. Listen to these "notes" later on to prepare for quizzes and exams.

- Auditory learners will benefit from tape-recording each class. Listening to tapes may be more useful than repeatedly reading written material.

Study tips for visual learners

- Your learning will be greatly enhanced by highlighting key phrases and sentences. (Don't fall into the trap of highlighting paragraphs; then you've just got lengthy text in a different color!)

- Use different colors of ink when taking notes for study purposes. For example, write one important list to memorize in green, another in red.

- As much as you're able to (depending upon the subject), visualize what you're reading.

- Make your notes more visually interesting and memorable by creating diagrams, and using arrows and circles to emphasize facts.

IMPROVING YOUR MEMORY

Students sometimes go on autopilot. They may be repeating facts aloud or reading words on a page, but part of their mind is elsewhere. Paying attention to what you're trying to learn is the first step in improving recall. If information never really got in, there's no way to retrieve it when you need it.

While you are studying or reading or quizzing yourself, mentally organize facts into meaningful groups. Long lists of facts are much easier to learn if they are grouped in a way that makes sense to you.

For example, when memorizing all 50 state capitals, sort them into geographic groupings: New England, the Mid-Atlantic states, the South, the Midwest, and so on.

Be selective in what you try to memorize: Determine what is most important, and then focus on learning those facts first.

Another good strategy is to associate what you're learning with facts you already know. The more you can associate a new fact with already familiar material, the more likely you'll be to recall it.

For example, if you are familiar with the geography of the southern states, you will be more likely to remember the story of Sherman's march through the South during the Civil War by visualizing the sweep of his troop movements superimposed on a map of the region.

BECOMING AN ACTIVE LEARNER

Many students study passively. They simply start at the beginning of a chapter and read through it, hoping to recall what they have read. They may highlight key words or phrases, but they do little else to actively learn the material.

An active learner, however, constantly works with the material. He or she repeatedly asks, "What does this remind me of? What can I associate this with in order to remember it? How can I say this in my own words? What is the main point?" Active learners engage with the material they are reading by summarizing, an activity that requires active engagement, rather than passively copying a phrase or sentence from the text.

Tips for active learning in class

- Sit in the front and middle of each class whenever possible. These are the "success seats," which help you pay attention and show your professor that you have come to learn.

- Develop a working relationship with each of your professors. Make sure they know you and what your needs are.

- Participate in class, make comments, and ask questions. The more you participate, the more you'll be interested in the class.

Tips for active learning when studying

- Skim the chapter to learn what it is generally about first. Then reread it.

- Turn chapter headings into questions. This will give you a focus when you read the chapter.

- After formulating your question, say it aloud (engaging your auditory as well as your visual brain), then answer the question aloud.

- After answering each question in the chapter, briefly review the major points, reading each heading aloud and attempting to recall points of information under it. Return to the material at a later time for a second review.

- Learn material backward and forward. For example, study from the word to the definition. Later, go from the definition to naming the word.

- Test yourself repeatedly at intervals of several hours.

- Try to explain the material to someone who knows nothing about it. See if you can answer their questions. Teaching someone else is an excellent way of learning yourself.

- Learn to "overlearn" by using lots of practice trials. After you seem to know all the material, you will need to develop overlearning strategies to be sure you have it in long-term storage.

CREATING EFFECTIVE STUDY ROUTINES

Plan to study in a distraction-free environment. For example, study alone in your dorm room or in the library. Some students find the open study rooms of a library distracting. Studying in a more remote area of the library such as the stacks or in an empty classroom may help those students. Some schools set aside quiet areas for study at night. Remember, "distraction-free" doesn't have to mean "quiet." In fact, some students report that they are better able to concentrate and ignore distractions if they listen to music while studying. The music provides a sound screen that shuts out distractions.

Divide your study time into short segments. It's generally not a good idea to set aside long periods of time to study before an exam. You'll learn more efficiently in shorter time periods during which you can truly concentrate.

Develop study routines. Weekday study routines should be developed around your schedule of classes and labs. On weekends, set aside regular times for study, for example, always on Saturday afternoons and Sunday evenings. That way you'll be less likely to make social plans during these times.

PREPARING FOR QUIZZES, EXAMS, MIDTERMS, AND FINALS

Test yourself to make sure that you really know the material. Many students confuse recognition memory with retrieval memory. That is, some students mistakenly assume that when information seems familiar, they know it. Recognizing and understanding material that is presented to you is not equivalent to being able to retrieve, organize, and explain that material.

One good strategy is to test yourself before an exam by creating study cards on 5x7 index cards. Write an important name, term, or date on one side of each card. Then, on the flip side of the card, write an explanation of the meaning or importance of that name, term, or date. Then quiz yourself by going through the cards, viewing only the short answer side of each card and challenging yourself to remember and explain the long answer on its reverse side. Each time you answer correctly, remove that card from the pile.

Continue cycling through the cards until you have given a correct answer for all of them. Now do the process in reverse: Look at each card from its long-answer side and quiz yourself to recall the short answer on its flip side.

Another good strategy is to form a study group. Many students benefit by studying with others. In a study group, you can check your understanding of the reading material through discussion with other students. This can be a good way to prepare for assignments as well as quizzes and exams, and really get a handle on required information. Be sure that you have chosen a group of students who are serious about studying. Go over as many problems or possible questions as you can. Take turns answering hypothetical questions or old test questions aloud. You may even write up a crib sheet detailing all the important topics and information covered in the course. If the test is a closed-book exam, be sure you know what's on the crib sheet. If it's an open-book exam, bring the sheet with you.

Whatever you do, do not stay up all night studying! Sleep deprivation can give students a double dose of ADHD symptoms, making memory retrieval even more difficult.

TAKING QUIZZES AND EXAMS

Many students with ADHD/LD find that even when they have studied hard, their performance on exams doesn't adequately reflect what they've learned. Poor test performance can stem from a variety of factors, including test anxiety, sleep deprivation, and memory-retrieval problems. Below are a number of strategies to help improve your test performance so that you'll have a better chance of demonstrating what you've learned.

- Arrange to have your exam schedule altered so that you don't have more than one final exam or midterm per day.

- Review the entire exam before you begin answering any question.

- Go through your exam once, answering all of the items that you're able to. Then return to the most challenging test items and devote the remaining time to them.

- Don't allow yourself to become so fixated on one short essay that you neglect to respond at all to the others.

- If you're not sure, go with your first guess.

If you are a student who experiences reading difficulties, there are a number of strategies you can use. First, ask your student support services office if you can have your texts and reading assignments recorded. The student support services office may offer this service free of charge. This service requires that you plan in advance. As a general rule, allow at least four to six weeks. Additionally, many textbooks are now available in audio formats (tape or CD) and may be offered free of charge to ADHD or LD students. See if this is possible with your books. Also consider purchasing software that allows you to scan in reading material, and then have your computer read the material aloud as you read the text on your computer screen.

It is always a good option to talk to your professor about your reading comprehension difficulties. Explain that multiple-choice questions are difficult for you to comprehend and answer. Many students with ADHD are such creative thinkers that they complicate multiple-choice questions by finding ways in which more than one answer can be correct. You can ask if it would be possible to take a short-answer test instead. If your professor will not allow a change in the test format, ask him or her to consider allowing you to explain your answer(s) on a separate sheet of paper. This will demonstrate that you were not simply guessing, but that you answered based on valid reasoning.

If your reading comprehension difficulties lead you to be unsure about the meaning of an exam question, don't hesitate to ask the professor to rephrase the question. (Such a request will usually receive a more accommodating response if you have informed the professor of your comprehension difficulties prior to the exam.) However, make sure this is an option beforehand, so you don't become anxious if the professor says "No" while you are taking the exam.

English composition classes, which are typically required on college campuses, can be daunting for students with written language problems. Such a class can be valuable in developing better writing skills. However, some composition classes require one paper per week. This can feel overwhelming, especially in combination with a full course load. Here are several strategies that can be helpful in dealing with a composition class:

1   Take a reduced course load during the term when you are enrolled in a composition class.

2   Research the requirements of the other classes that you plan to take to make sure that none of them require papers as well.

3   Work closely with a writing tutor from the first week of class so that you can keep up with demanding writing requirements.

4   Consider working with an ADHD coach who can help you allocate your time among the demands of your composition class, the work required by your other classes, and the tasks of daily living.

5   Use word processing software when writing your papers. By using spell-checker and grammar-checker functions, proofreading can be done directly on the computer. This eliminates the possibility of introducing errors in your final copy.

6   Have a tutor or someone in the campus writing lab routinely review and explain all writing assignments before you prepare your first draft. Ask him or her also to review your revised drafts and then your final papers.

OVERCOMING PROCRASTINATION

Procrastination can be the biggest enemy to accomplishment. Students procrastinate for several reasons: low motivation, fear of failure, difficulty getting started, or feeling overwhelmed. Let's look at some ways to combat these factors.

LOW MOTIVATION

Many students put off assignments in classes that don't interest them. Students with ADHD or LD are no exception. It is essential that you select a major that excites you and that is compatible with your strengths and weaknesses. That way, you have lots of classes that interest you.

However, even with the selection of an appropriate major, there will be required courses that may hold less interest for you. You need to find ways to motivate yourself to work in these courses. Use fun or relaxing activities as rewards for completing particularly unpleasant or difficult tasks such as:

- Going to get a soft drink or snack.
- Making a phone call.
- Visiting a friend or roommate.
- Taking a walk.
- Watching a little TV.

Schedule bigger rewards at the end of your day. For example, "If I get all the way through all the planned activities in my day planner, I'll go out with my friends to a movie tonight."

Even larger rewards can be scheduled for bigger accomplishments: "When I finish my political science term paper, I'll go away for the weekend."

Be sure to give yourself a time limit because these short breaks can easily turn into long ones. If you find that a 15-minute break often turns into a 60-minute break, set a timer for yourself and then get back to work.

FEAR OF FAILURE

Some students with ADHD or LD can feel overwhelmed by college courses or assignments, especially at first. They sometimes put off beginning a project because they wonder if they are capable of completing it. Some ways of combating this are:

- Ask for feedback from your tutor or counselor to assess whether your fear is realistic.

- Get started. The longer you put it off, the bigger it will look as the deadline nears.

- Talk to your professor. Tell him or her that you need help.

- Go to your tutor and ask for help on the project; share your concerns so the tutor can give you clarifying feedback.

DIFFICULTY GETTING STARTED

Many students fear they will appear dumb if they tell their tutor or professor they do not know how to get started. Don't be afraid to ask. Talk to your professor to be sure you understand the project. Then go to your tutor and ask for help in planning the project. Let your tutor know that you are having trouble getting started and ask for suggestions on how to overcome this problem.

When the task looks big, divide and conquer! Break the task down into as many small pieces as you can think of. Write each task down as a to-do item in your day planner. Cross out each item you finish. Seeing all the things crossed off a list will give you a sense of accomplishment. As you begin your ascent of the big project, don't look at the top of the hill, that is, don't look at everything you will have to do. Just look at the next small step on your to-do list.

ORGANIZING YOUR STUDY SPACE

Any task is harder when you are disorganized. If you are having trouble getting your work done, try some of these approaches.

1   Clear off your desk surface. A cluttered, disorganized work space can be much harder to work in; a clean, neat desk top can help you feel calmer and more focused.

2   Gather all of the materials you will need. Make a list, then get all your supplies together so you won't have to keep stopping (or be tempted to socialize as you wander down the hall to borrow a stapler or computer paper).

3   Make a task list. Often students jump into a task with no advance planning. This can lead to confusion and inefficiency, so always make a list of what you need to do.

If organizing your study space and dorm room are difficult for you, it may be helpful to hire a professional organizer to get your space in order and to develop systems for keeping it organized. An ADHD coach can help you with this as well.

RESISTING TEMPTATIONS

On many college campuses, there is active partying four or more nights a week. In addition, there are daily temptations: to join the conversation down the hall, to go out for a pizza with your roommate, and so on.

If socializing instead of studying is a temptation, you may want to select a school with a less social atmosphere. Or once at school, choose friends who are motivated and who study before they party. If you are tempted to socialize when you study where you live, go to the library or to an isolated study area.

If going to sleep is a temptation, don't study in or near your bed. Likewise, if staying up late is a temptation, set a "reverse alarm clock," an alarm that reminds you to get ready to go to sleep. Students with ADHD or LD can get caught up in the activity of the moment and lose track of time.

If you are tempted to skip classes, ask yourself why. Is it because it is an early-morning class? Should you avoid signing up for 8 a.m. or 9 a.m. classes when possible? Is it because the class meets on Friday afternoons and you are always tempted to leave early for the weekend? Are you skipping class because you are ill prepared? Bored? Rather than simply making a resolution to quit skipping class, try to understand what is going on in order to find the best solution for you. If you have trouble figuring this out yourself, you might talk with a counselor or your college counseling center to gain some insights.

MINIMIZING DISTRACTIONS

Distractibility is often a problem for ADHD/LD students. Dorm life is especially distracting. The noise level in many dorms is high and often goes on into the early-morning hours. Discuss your distractibility with the student support services office when you are applying to each school; see what suggestions they have for coping with this in college.

For example, some schools have "quiet dorms" with rules banning loud music or conversation after a certain hour in the evening. Or you may want to sign up for a single dorm room so that you are not distracted by a roommate. As an upperclassman, you may want to live off-campus in a quieter environment.

If you have no choice but to live in a noisy dorm environment, you will need to find a quiet study place. If you have trouble finding one, discuss the problems with the student support services office. Headphones can be helpful for some students; the quiet, calming music screens out distracting noises. Other tips that may help include:

- Tape-record lectures or get access to a complete set of lecture notes provided by the professor or by a fellow student.
  Or use a note-taking service. A note-taker is a very common accommodation at most schools. This is also useful for students who have auditory processing difficulties or are unable to write quickly enough to take good notes.

- Sign up for small classes when possible for better concentration and fewer distractions.

- Sit away from a window or door that may be distracting.

- Actively participate in class discussions to increase your concentration.

- Sit in front of the classroom if that helps you pay better attention.

REDUCING FRUSTRATIONS

Students with ADHD or LD sometimes struggle with low frustration tolerance. You may find yourself feeling so frustrated that you tend to give up on a difficult task. As frustration level rises, ability to solve problems decreases.

You may want to discuss your frustration with a tutor or counselor. It is also helpful to understand it better and learn coping skills to increase your frustration tolerance. Ask yourself the following questions:

1   Am I frustrated because my ADHD/LD issues sometimes require me to work harder than other students?

2   What can I do to discharge these frustrations in a good way?

3   Do I understand the task?

4   Am I frustrated because I need a tutor or some structured assistance?

5   Would it be better to study with another student in the class?

6   Do I need moral support? Would I feel better if I talked to other students in the class about how they are approaching the assignment?

7   Should I work on this course in smaller bites because it is so difficult for me?

8 Is this course too hard for me? Have I made a poor selection or received poor advice in choosing this course?

9 Should I drop this course?

Don't jump to this last conclusion first. Many students with ADHD or LD drop courses they could have completed successfully if only they had some tutorial help, and some help in working through the reasons for their frustration.

JOINING A STUDENT SUPPORT GROUP

Many students find it helpful to join an ADHD/LD student support group. If your school doesn't have such a group, consider forming one. You may need to work with your advisor or find an active faculty sponsor for the group to continue successfully. Such a group will not only offer good emotional support, it can also become a source of information regarding courses, professors, and study tips. Occasionally your student services office may form a student panel to educate the faculty about the needs of students with ADHD/LD. You could participate in this too.

Don't hide your learning or attention problem from friends and faculty. Hiding it helps perpetuate the misconception that ADHD or LD means you are not as smart as others. That of course is not the case!

TAKING PART IN
EXTRACURRICULAR ACTIVITIES

The opportunity to participate in extracurricular activities is an important aspect of your college experience. Making friends, building leadership and social skills, developing your athletic ability, and increasing your self-confidence are some of the many reasons why extracurricular activities can be important.

It is easy to become overcommitted in college. Try to guard against it. If you choose to join a sorority or fraternity, for example, the time commitment will be large. Participation in team athletics and other clubs likewise requires a big time commitment. This goes hand in hand with good time management.

Whatever your extracurricular activities are, use time-management techniques as you go through the process of committing to outside activities. Using your day planner or other organizing system, block out time that is already committed: class time, tutor appointments, study time, meals, sleep, and relaxation.

Once you have blocked out your committed time, carefully assess whether you have the time and effort for the club, sport, or social activity you are considering. If you decide to play a sport that demands both afternoon practice and weekend games, you may have to cut back on your weekend social life. Is this a trade-off you want to make? If your realistic answer is "Yes," go ahead with the commitment.

Try to build in the right level of stimulation. Some students with ADHD or LD find they function best when they are busy and when their days are structured. Such students may discover that they waste more time and procrastinate more when they have large blocks of free time. Other students feel too stressed if most of their time is structured and committed. It may take you a couple of semesters to learn what your best patterns are. You may already have a good idea of what works best for you from your high school experience.

BEING EMPLOYED PART-TIME

Many students need to work in order to pay for all or part of their college expenses. You should be realistic about your energy level, organization level, study requirements, and time availability when making a work commitment.

Most students with ADHD or LD take a reduced course load of 12 hours or fewer per semester. If finances require you to work, you may need to reduce your course load to 9. In many schools, 12 hours constitutes a full-time load, but a student is classified as part-time if he or she takes fewer hours than that.

You will need to discuss this requirement with the schools you are considering. In many schools, full-time status is required to participate in certain campus activities or to live on campus.

Consider on-campus jobs. Generally, on-campus jobs are more convenient and preferable to off-campus jobs, even though they may pay less. Working on campus will help you feel integrated into the college community and will offer you another way to make friends. Supervisors of student employees working on campus will be more understanding if you need to take time off to study for finals. An off-campus employer may be far less supportive and understanding if you need time off.

Look for other ways to deal with financial needs. If money is a concern, you may want to investigate other ways to reduce your expenses. Students who enjoy taking an advisory role with younger college students (or have an interest in leadership positions) may want to consider becoming a resident advisor (RA) in a dormitory. Often free housing is offered to RAs in exchange for functioning as a counselor and advisor for underclassmen.

CHAPTER SUMMARY

• • • The key to your college success is to work step-by-step to develop good life management habits.

• • • Good time management is essential. It's important to learn to use a day planner and to break assignments and long-term projects into small steps that can be scheduled in your planner every day.

• • • Work on learning how to become a more efficient learner. Know your best learning style, and learn better ways to prepare for tests and exams.

• • • Become an active learner. Participate in class and actively engage yourself in reading and studying in order to better learn the material.

• • • Identify the problems that repeatedly get in your way, such as procrastination, fear of failure, memory difficulties, getting distracted, and build the techniques discussed in this chapter to combat them.

CONCLUSION

Wonderful opportunities for college students with ADHD or LD are out there for you. By choosing a college that is a good match for your needs and preferences, you'll be off to a positive start. Supports and accommodations provided by colleges for students with special learning challenges are better than ever before. Then, make sure that you get the support you need from advisors, professors, tutors, coaches, and counselors. Take advantage of career counseling and academic advising to choose a career path that taps into your strengths and focuses on your interests.

There are many success strategies outlined in this book. Consider each of them and choose the ones that seem the best match for you. With this college survival guide to help you chart your course, you are on your way to a great college experience.

RESOURCES
FOR COLLEGE STUDENTS
WITH ADHD AND LD

GETTING READY TO APPLY FOR COLLEGE

Taymans, J. M., West, L. L., & Sullivan, M. (Eds.) (2000). *Unlocking potential: College and other choices for people with LD and ADHD.* Bethesda, MD: Woodbine House.

VonGruben, J. F. (1999). *College countdown: The parent's and student's survival kit for the college admissions process.* New York: McGraw-Hill.

COLLEGE GUIDES
HELPFUL TO STUDENTS WITH ADHD OR LD

Asher, D. (2000). *Cool colleges: For the hyper-intelligent, self-directed, late blooming, and just plain different.* Berkeley, CA: Ten Speed.

Kaplan (2005). *Unofficial, unbiased guide to the 331 most interesting colleges, 2005 edition.* New York: Author.

Kravetz, M., & Wax, I. F. (2005). *K & W guide to colleges for students with learning disabilities or attention deficit disorder (8th ed.).* New York: Princeton Review.

Petersons (2003). *Colleges for students with learning disabilities or ADD.* Lawrenceville, NJ: Author.

Pope, L. (2000). *Colleges that change lives: 40 schools you should know about even if you're not a straight-A student.* New York: Penguin.

Scheiber, B., & Talpers, J. (1987). *Unlocking potential: College and other choices for learning-disabled people: A step-by-step guide.* Chevy Chase, MD: Adler & Adler.

SURVIVING AND THRIVING IN COLLEGE AS A STUDENT WITH ADHD OR LD

Bramer, J. S. (1996). *Succeeding in college with attention deficit disorders: Issues & strategies for students, counselors & educators.* Plantation, FL: Specialty.

Cobb, J. (2001). *Learning how to learn: Getting into and surviving college when you have a learning disability.* Atlanta, GA: Child Welfare League of America.

Dolber, R. (1996). *College and career success for students with learning disabilities.* Lincolnwood, IL: VGM Career Horizons.

McConnell, K., Ryser, G., & Higgins, J. (2000). *Practical ideas that really work for students with ADHD: With evaluation form.* Austin, TX: Pro-Ed.

Mooney, J., & Cole, D. (2000). *Learning outside the lines: Two Ivy League students with learning disabilities and ADHD give you the tools for academic success and educational revolution.* New York: Fireside.

Quinn, P. O., Ratey, N. A., & Maitland, T. L. (2000). *Coaching college students with AD/HD.* Silver Spring, MD: Advantage.

Quinn, P. O. (2001). *ADD and the college student: A guide for high school and college students with attention deficit disorder.* Washington, D.C.: Magination Press.

Robinson, A. (1993). *What smart students know: Maximum grades. Optimum learning. Minimum time.* New York: Random House.